AN ORDINARY DAY

To Susan —

All good wishes,

Diane

Enjoy,

AN ORDINARY DAY

Poems by Diane Marquart Moore
Photography by Victoria I. Sullivan

To Rose Anne Raphael, artist extraordinaire

You can find something truly important in an ordinary minute... Mitch Alborn

CONTENT

ALSO BY DIANE MARQUART MOORE

POETRY
     Field Marks
     Consolation of Gardens
     Ultimate Pursuit
     All Love,
     Let the Trees Answer
     Spring's Kiss
     Above the Prairie
     Sifting Red Dirt
     A Slow Moving Stream
     Street Sketches
     Corner of Birch Street
     Strand of Beads
     A Lonely Grandmother
     Between Plants and Humans
     Night Offices
     Departures
     In a Convent Garden
     Mystical Forest
     Everything is Blue
     Post Cards From Diddy Wah Diddy
     Alchemy
     Old Ridges
     Rising Water
     The Holy Present and Farda
     Grandma's Good War
     Afternoons in Oaxaca (Las Poesias)
     The Book of Uncommon Poetry
     Counterpoint
     Your Chin Doesn't Want to Marry

Soaring
More Crows
Just Passing Through
Moment Seized

YOUNG ADULTS
Martin and the Last Tribe
Martin Finds His Totem
Flood on the Rio Teche
Sophie's Sojourn in Persia
Kajun Kween
Martin's Quest

ADULT FICTION
Redeemed by Blood
Silence Never Betrays
Chant of Death with Isabel Anders
Goat Man Murder
The Maine Event
Nothing for Free

CHILDREN
The Beast Beelzebufo
The Cajun Express

NON-FICTION
Porch Posts with Janet Faulk-Gonzales
Iran: In A Persian Market
Their Adventurous Will
Live Oak Gardens
Treasures of Avery Island

COLORS

A fat coon stopped his climb
in an oak beside the coulee,
stared at me as if he knew
I'd been to some California pageant,

a grand expedition to the desert scape

of Joshua trees, their arms covered
by sudden, impermanent snow,
the north wind blowing generous powder.
In that desert I couldn't escape the glare
of light, ice streaking our hotel windows,

heaven bursting with a tumult of white
in a place of white supremacy
that sent me back to a masked coon
climbing an oak beside the coulee,
perfectly balanced and welcoming me home.

I think he possessed prescience,
knew why I'd gone so far,
spending myself on a restless journey
to see my grandchildren's brown skin
glowing with their mother's love…
an unlikely justice sealed.

CLOSE CALL

I could forgive your shoes lying everywhere,
sterling silver spoons battered and stained
from your constant cups of coffee and tea,
your thinking a bed needs no making after sleep,
sharing with me a life of small annoyances.

But I could not forgive this threat,
death thrown to us by accidental x-ray,
one that showed pebbled aliens in your chest
my awakening to mistrust and the sound
of angels in the distance.

I went outdoors, the weather predicted
as south wind and 60-degree temps
and began sweeping the patio,
trying to clear away fear that persisted,
blood rushing at my feet.

On the street, windows of the curious opened,
the underworld strained to take you away
like the last judgement
in a morning of nameless stars,
but I kept sweeping, sweeping.

The wind shifted north unexpectedly,
and I stood in the briskness of a peak moment
alert to sound, crows screaming
as they dove from the sky
wild with life in an ecstatic interim,

every terror swept away
leaving an unaltered pledge to eternity.

Our lives would not be haunted.
You would go on making the world…
for me.

THE DEATH OF A
DIAMOND

Yesterday I thought of Elizabeth Bishop's poem
about losing things, the one advising us

to practice losing something every day
when I lost the diamond from Godmother's
engagement ring, a *something*

lost *somewhere* in Barnes and Noble,
a bookstore I haunt weekly with holiday cards.
I envision the inherited diamond
being found by some book-starved patron
who hadn't the wherewithal

to buy even one volume.
The sparkling gem had to have given itself up
to the poetry or essay sections
between poems by W. S. Merwin
and essays by Ursula LeGuin,

both of which I later purchased.
The diamond could have purposely loosened
and ejected itself at the cashier's station
where I also bought three newspapers
and claimed a free cookie

overwhelmed with caramel
and chips of white chocolate diamonds,
my greed signaling New Year's resolutions.
The chip diamonds on either side
of this ring with its antique setting

remain intact and warn me
not to value expensive possessions
although the vision remains:
Godmother lying in her tall tester bed
an old waif propped against plump pillows

posed in self-imposed exile to invalidness,
a woman who stored at least ten diamond rings
in a Blackburg, Virginia vault
along with her delicate health,
disowned me when I divorced a violent man.

The loss of this gleaming stone reminded me
that Victorian expectations of eternal marriage
would never have been met by me,
and the last of her hauteur now departs
with a $4,000 diamond her spouse passed on...

Clearly not *your* engagement, St. Anthony* says.

*Patron saint of lost *somethings*.

SISTER MARY ZITA
DEPARTS

Chimes above my patio swing wildly,
ringing *Sanctus* in a north wind,

music that routs a resident crow
hiding under the eaves,

his dark voice strangely silent.
Death captures Mary Zita's eyes

bright as flowers she cut for the altar...
this morning uninhabited by joy.

Corridors empty out her screams
as she embraces the air,

ends her journey
at the top of my tall camellia

known to birth only pink blossoms.
But a red one, as foreordained as her Call,

now dispels rain and gloom
and I know it is Sister saying farewell.

She has put away her woolen cap
of woven stars, her earth-time crown,

and I will not cut the red flower
knowing vagrant ones will increase.

I will say thank you for that flower
and for the flower who kissed my hand at The
Peace,

whose *thank you* was the only English she spoke;
her only dream... the garden of Paradise.

SISTER MARY ZITA II.

The tree planted by godfather Markham
never fertilized, fortified in any way

save by sun and rain,
each January puts forth
pink and hearty blossoms
for desk and table,
plays watchman over coons,
possums, armadillo, even snakes
lurking in the coulee beyond,
blooms through shadow and storm,
bliss and suffering,
glistening with morning dew,
sturdy in spring winds,
petals outspread,
overcome with love of this earth
without a patient gardener;
one vagabond red bloom willing to follow
Sr. Mary Zita into the Also World.

SISTER MARY ZITA III.

This is the time of camellias
blooming before their time,
Mary Zita's red one of farewell
topping a tree with blooms

unparalleled for a quarter century,
their two unlikely fellow gardeners
deceased but still gardening —
Markham, Victorian elitist
and his pink blossoms,
Mary Zita, Filipino refugee
and her hybrid red one —
their colors entwining.
Wind comes out of the north
and not a blossom drops.
The sound of the Southern Pacific
carries on the wind, shakes the ground
of a ginger plant by the drive
trying to rival camellia blooms;
but these winter flowers tell us
they are beauties of nowhere,
have stolen the light from another sky,
from seasons not yet given…
the scent of things changing.

SCENE ON HWY 182

I glimpsed him as we sped by,
a man enclosed in the false spring,
temperatures rising,
light flowing through naked trees.
He sat on bare ground,
empty syrup bucket disappeared,
his pole bent in mid-air.

I could not see his face
turned to the stream
as the first catfish of the season
struggled in ditch water
murky as the Bayou Teche.
I envisioned the old man's pirogue
gliding silently under the bridge,

him returning to water
remote from receding shore,
waiting there and dreaming of dead forms —
friends playing Blue Grass, Chanky Chank,
as they tapped their calloused feet
on clouds of morning fog.
He may have been praying

for summer to come,
or thinking of the journeys of unsettled
ancestors
wild and outraged at rising water
and its weight,
or simply of the fish
coming up out of the water
turning over and over

and that night quieted
in a black iron skillet
sizzling with much-used oil
or in plates on his kitchen table,
accompanied by hush puppies, beer,
the awed look of his family
as the fish became what it was made for.

TRUMP'S WAR I.

What is left of Christmas,
the red glow of a poinsettia
living without water;
two white candles blown out.
Dark edges belie things extinguished,
leaves in the yard cling to ground
like the debris of missile strikes.
A strident voice thinks itself important

proclaiming Iran the war of wars,
dares us to speak evil of him
as he explodes the Last Judgement.
He raises the Stars and Stripes
on land he does not own,
roams the Mideast,
orange hair afire,
trumpeting sour notes of Taps,
boots burrowing deeply
into the sands of human ash,
bellowing *Respice ad finem* *.

Look to the end.

TRUMP'S WAR II.

His bugle call inspires crowd chaos.
At a funeral procession in Kerman
they remove their shoes,
encumbering robes,
stampede each other,
fifty people die frenzied deaths.
They join General Soleimani
in Islam's Paradise, chanting

Death to the U.S.
strike up the band,
hallowed be a long-awaited war.
Rumi tells the left behind
not to cry *alas*
when their brothers are gone
and they visit the gravesites;
their brothers, like Rumi,
swiftly passed through a flimsy curtain,
released from this falsehood —
a buffoon annihilating himself
and our world dishonored.

LE GRANDE EMMERDANT

I cherish this friend
whose explanations
of misfortune
sometimes puzzle me.

However he is
a fine poet
and an expert
in languaging STUFF

so when he says
"Our rhythms have changed"
followed by
"Life is many-textured,"

I interpret
some *stuff*
has happened
and he and his wife

have had to revise their
schedule for living
peacefully and
he doesn't want to talk

about IT,
IT being the *stuff*
because verbalizing IT
may multiply IT

or divide IT
and make more,

whatever...
but I don't know

what to pray for
when I think of his misfortunes.
"That's ok,"
his wife says,

"I just say 'Dear God
take care of IT
everywhere and for
everyone in the world'

and IT is covered
when I say that.
IT means just that...
I'm not lying

when I say
'I'm praying for you.'
Actually," she adds,
"in the morning

I say to myself 'I'm awake'
and that means
stuff may happen
but I'm still here

living the many-textured
life that, like an Oriental carpet
is filled with knots,
no use to remind my mate

It is often
full of IT."

ABOUT FUTURE FAME

Literary critics say a poet
should never write poetry
about writing a poem
and so I defy the Academy
with this poem about poetry.

When they discover my poems
too late for me to enjoy readers

but not too late
for one reader who comes
upon them by chance

in a dusty second-hand bookstore;
paperbacks curled up
as if in deep sleep
but not deceased,
language untouched;

they will find powerful work
merely a semi-colon away,
a brief pause,
not an end period,
waiting for a discerning interpolator.

THE FACE OF FACEBOOK OR I LOVE ME

I know I'm not the only person
who questions why she's on facebook

preaching and bragging the agenda
of each day, a spreadsheet of narcissism

that must make my ancestors cringe
who counseled us to practice modesty

and believed that pride goes
before a public fall. But Jesus saves.

Here's the latest photo of myself
and, oh, my grandchildren also;

Here's me five years ago
and don't I still look good?

I've just published an-award winning book
and someone in New York left me a message

I know must be a bow of national recognition
for my latest novel about all my tragedies.

A bark and a meow for photos of Zip and Kitty,
beloved pets lying on cushions of compassion.

Here's my 25th wedding anniversary photo
and we're still madly in love,

notice how he looks into my eyes

and tells me how I haven't changed.

Here's a list of all the foods I consume
despite the doctors telling me

to lose 50 or more pounds that does not show
in my face but remains on a rear end not shown.

I'm just a perfect amaryllis
advertising myself each morning

and hoping you'll be half as admirable
when you're my age

bathing in the eternal fountain of youth
and self-loving beauty.

AT BREAKFAST

Purple curls in a vase on the dining table,
the lonely hyacinth smells of funerals
and looks like a gossipy old woman
still perming her hair but not talking.

Some deep absences send me looking
for old friends in a place of grief —
dead leaves heaped in a backyard
covering what rain has not ravaged.

The language of flowers and trees
and a blue sky emptied of clouds
I think of as poetry without lines
that realize their inventiveness and passion.

GLASS ART

Angels live in my glass pieces,
guardians of the Spirit
that began it all
flown in to set up residence
in stained glass and stone;
out of darkness beating their wings
and hovering around me
so immersed in fading life.
They make each hour holy,
gleaming memories of childhood —
purple cupola of grandmother's house,
a porch's red roof looking out
on desert and full grown forest,
red hills of Mississippi ancestry,
the prize, a bare tree
overlooking a field of gold flowers…
the luster of humility.

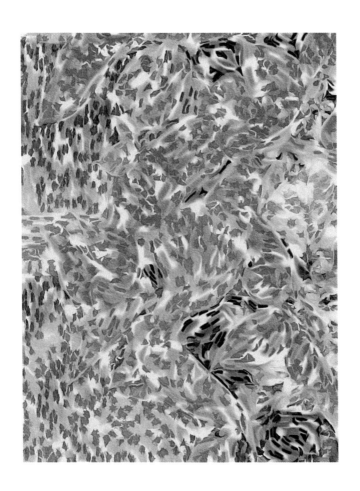

INSOMNIA

At night I travel the road to childhood,
a long lane leading to school rooms,
teachers startled not at what I know
but what I feel
already wishing away sensitivity,
vague insights,

imagined abandonment.
I awake to sounds of rain pattering,
look out at muddy bottoms of water gathering,
remember that in the night I dreamed
my older brother pushed and held
my youngest brother's face under water.
I rescued him, hoping he might see
how beauty arises from persistence —
the poinsettia. abandoned after Christmas,
a convincing story of longevity
astonishing with its heavy blooms,
a red brilliance on the hearth,
reminding me that seeding and sowing
would soon grow over ill-fated secrets.

A SUNDAY APHORISM

Churchgoing:

Not to see Him

but to be seen by them.

AGAIN, CAMELLIAS

Today's rain does not dishearten
pink and red blooms,
another winter midnight survived;
the miracle of a camellia's secluded growth
blushes in the window again.
I hear Godfather Markham singing
planting songs, rites of isolation
while his world perishes.
He waits for the new year,
learning how to die at 99 1/2 years,
looking out at a camellia's self-sufficiency.
Just another thunder storm, he says,
old age settles in beyond our sight,
beyond the bloom of vanity.

TO THE OBESE

You are the victim of your own desire:
broken hip, bent back, knee surgeries.
You're told you live on a razor
that seeks to attack your jiggling flesh.
but you seem to have fallen among the blind,
mirrors reflecting a fat doll face
you call pre-raphaelite beauty.
All seasons lead you to a laden table
and flesh layers itself even in lean times.
You try to live by camouflage
that cannot cover the greed,
hopeless case if ever…
hiding in the underground of weight.
I would place a flower
on the grave's mound of flesh
but fear a hand would reach out
from the cave of the Also World,
seeking after-dinner dessert.

THE DAY AFTER DISCOVERING A DAUGHTER'S CONTINUED ADDICTION

Thank God I'm addicted to books
poetry and all imaginings
beyond the suffering of my addict daughter
now wired with circuity that takes her away
from life and what she could have had:
the cord of trust.

READING THE WORK OF OBSCURE POETS

So strange, the democratic venture
a sleek volume of American poets
from doggerel to sonnet,
songs of unrecognized and famous,
fury, laud, preface and lengthy ode,
a medley of illuminations
and grace notes in an unforgiving world.

Here, the scant successes and downfalls
of obscure poets like celestial beings
never read aloud,
I see gates with bars on them,
dreams deferred, unfinished and distant.
For example, Lorine Niedecker
a Black Hawk Island poet,

one who scrubbed floors in a hospital,
a woman without presumption
or desire for competition
who made covenant with poetry;
and if I were Ogden Nash
I'd write something like this about her:
"there's purity in obscurity."

She built a rude cabin on the island
to hold her solitude, wrote about Darwin,
how he defined the universe by law
and left the details up to all poets —
our puny attempts to leave signatures on time.
And after a reading in Grand Coteau
last evening, a poet laureate

said of the readers included:
They all took their work seriously.
I wasn't there but, yes,
53 years of writing poems —
seriously—and still counting,
still writing, hoping for a democratic
Vol. III of *American Poetry.*

VISIT WITH A VERSIFIER

I speak of something true
I could never do

make rhymes that often appease and inspire —
with doggerel lyrics I yet tread a thin wire;

but yesterday while visiting on a gray winter day
a seldom sad versifier began to inveigh.

with rhyming verses of her choice,
moment by moment becoming a stronger voice;

light suddenly filtering into the room
cancelling our stories that had made the gloom,

throwing to the shadows former losses and fear
reading verses of nonsense that brought cheer;

Inspired, we went to the Chamber of Commerce
and without any plan or type of rehearse

read pop-up poems to an audience of five
happy for listeners who appreciated a live show;

and that is as inspirational a verse as I can write
one that *may* rhyme without sounding trite?

MARDI GRAS, ASH WEDNESDAY...
AND MORE RHYMING ATTEMPTS

Purple, yellow, green and blue
in the center, a fleur de lis,
each year the same hues
a dance of abandon and glee;

I opt for Wednesday's black ashes
to mark what is within

the bad karma in two slashes
of ever-dying sin.

They can have their brief cheer
but I will take the spirit's fall,
an elegy for the dark years
leading to the light of all in all.

MORNING

Once you begin writing rhyming verse, the
process has a lingering effect. The lines of free
verse become almost an embarrassment,
although the song of rhyme is less profound.
The answer to good poetics must be somewhat
like my mother's handwriting, which was a
hybrid, a combination of cursive and block
printing. The verses I produce, although
doggerel, dominate nighttime thinking, and
when I awaken, I am forgetful, drink a glass of
orange juice and don't realize I've drunk it. My
world is tilted until the savior of all thought —
coffee — brings me into focus. The terrible eyes
of the nighttime soul are closed again,
nightmares gone — and I look straight into the
sun, am alive in the light, although it is still far
off.

FLOODGATES

To address Robert Frost's question
will the world end in fire or ice?
in all probability we'll return to Noah's dilemma,
the earth surrounded by water,
soils desperate in Arizona?
southern California? even Louisiana?;
Today there are brown rivers in the yard,
bayous of no name,
patios flooding St. Francis's feet,
but he's unmoved
by catastrophes of climate,
the gray stone grows darker each month
his deathless heart imbedded in stone
still beats, birds land on his head
in mad gales, hail, and endless rain.
He's (God) mad at us
the Cajun woman in the meat market
rolls her eyes and prophesies,
and we're going to be washed away.
All because Speaker of the House Pelosi
tore President Trump's State of the Union
speech into equal lying pieces —
not even passed off as half truths—
we *will* be punished by weather.

BUGLE CALL

When I was a child of the Great War
I believed in the songs of hope for my country
and the day they rang in The Armistice
we turned a dial on the big Bendix radio
from battle news to "Let's Pretend;"
peace would be "everlasting,"
happiness "forever,"
and nothing — no thing —
would ever be rationed again...
especially brotherly love.
I am now eighty-five and "Let's Pretend"
long ago died a painful death,
leaving us to shudder in the sound of Taps
after four years of Trumpian rule,
to grapple with such things
as "real identity" driver's licenses —
proof that I have lived on this soil
for 85 years in a now-moribund democracy.

FROM THE HEAVENS

Rain falls in the night,
advancing water covering the midnight moon;
A pale flickering over the coulee
illuminates a coon solemnly crossing,
and from the Also World, Grandfather Paul
steps, smelling of car grease, gasoline:
products of his trade.
"Henry's Made A Lady of Lizzie,"
he sings, proud of his enterprise,
The Automobile… A pioneer,
he stands on an ancient running board,
thinks he's driving away from floods
in backwater towns, accelerating hope,
shows people how to escape,
decamp for roads, even muddy,
leading to the main route in a sacred sky.

ANOTHER FALSE SPRING DAY I

Old men show their white hair,
spring clover in February pushing through;
indoors, reading Basho by lamp light

I see snow-capped Mt. Fuji,
my life in a bundle on the poet's back.

ANOTHER FALSE SPRING DAY II.

If I had been Basho, I would
have written of midnight train whistles
in the night comforted
by thoughts of passengers
safe, warm within the cars;
but Basho walked everywhere,
a countryman but not provincial,
stopping at temporary hermitages,
seeking always the downpour
of cherry blossoms
and the fresh spring rain,
his sieges: mosquitoes, fleas, lice —
small wonder he praised all nature —
seeking artistic elegance.

MAINTENANCE

Useless to sweep a garden
in a temporal world,
the old camellia blooms,
untended,
its memory indifferent to season.
And what is this ancestral urge
to own land, house,
everything on loan
to keep warm, to clean,
sweep and mop, paint and repair?
All is already blessing.
Sun-drenched leaves
sway in a north wind,
St. Francis hovers nearby,
abandoned,
clutching a lamb, a Bible,
declares nature's blessings,
life on the road, maintenance free.

FENCE LINES

Broken slats in a fence lean forward,
a rope around one neck,
Mardi Gras beads encircling another.
Laden branches once drooped over
the weathered gray boards.
We snatched succulent fruit
but the planter died of cancer
and someone, perhaps his wife,

cut the branches back
now no fruit overhangs
for our blatant picking.
crescent moons shine above,
beaming on her ungraciousness —
someone lonely for the planter
but unwilling to share —
and the orange tree remains aloof,
carrying the sour scent of poverty.

AUTHOR

Diane Marquart Moore is a poet, journalist, an author of fiction and nonfiction, and a blogger at "A Word's Worth." She regularly contributes to the *Pinyon Review*, has published in *The Southwestern Review Interdisciplinary Humanities* (University of Louisiana, Lafayette, Louisiana), *The Xavier Review, Acadiana Profile Magazine, American Weave, Louisiana Historical Review, Trace,* among others. During the reign of the Shahanshah in Iran, she reviewed books and wrote articles for The *Yaddasht Haftegy* (The National Iranian Oil Company journal) in Ahwaz. She retired as archdeacon of the Episcopal Diocese of Western Louisiana and divides her time between Sewanee, Tennessee and New Iberia, Louisiana.

PHOTOGRAPHER

Victoria I. Sullivan is a writer, botanist, and photographer. She studied biology at the University of Miami, earned a Ph.D. in biology from Florida State University and held a faculty position in the Department of Biology at the University of Louisiana, Lafayette for 20 years. She has published poetry, flash fiction, many botanical papers and other nonfiction, and two speculative fiction sequels, *Adoption* and *Rogue Genes*, and a book for nature enthusiasts, *Why Water Plants Don't Drown*. Sullivan is a resident of Sewanee, Tennessee, and winters in New Iberia, Louisiana.

**We hope you
enjoyed reading
this Border
Press book**

If you would like to read more books and ebooks of poetry by Diane Marquart Moore, please email victoria@borderpressbooks.com to subscribe to our mailing list. Also, please go to www.borderpressbooks.com to learn about books in other genre published by Border Press Books.

Made in the USA
Columbia, SC
05 June 2020